Lea Michele

ABDO
Publishing Company

Big Buddy BOOKS
Buddy Bios

by **Sarah Tieck**

VISIT US AT
www.abdopublishing.com

Published by ABDO Publishing Company, 8000 West 78th Street, Edina, Minnesota 55439.

Printed in the United States of America, North Mankato, Minnesota.
102010
012011
 PRINTED ON RECYCLED PAPER

Coordinating Series Editor: Rochelle Baltzer
Contributing Editors: Megan M. Gunderson, BreAnn Rumsch, Marcia Zappa
Graphic Design: Maria Hosley
Cover Photograph: *AP Photo*: Gregg DeGuire/PictureGroup via AP IMAGES.
Interior Photographs/Illustrations: *AP Photo*: Vince Bucci (p. 27), Vince Bucci/Fox/PictureGroup via AP IMAGES
   (p. 25), Kristie Bull/Graylock.com (pp. 13, 16), Jeff Christensen (p. 19), Gregg DeGuire/PictureGroup via AP
   IMAGES (p. 23), Adam Nadel (p. 9) Chris Pizzello (pp. 21, 23, 28); *Getty Images*: Richard Corkery/NY Daily
   Archive via Getty Images (p. 15), Charley Gallay/Getty Images for Fox (p. 5), Bruce Glikas/FilmMagic
   (pp. 6, 14), Hulton Archive (p. 13), Tom Wargacki/WireImage (p. 10).

Library of Congress Cataloging-in-Publication Data

Tieck, Sarah, 1976-
  Lea Michele : star of glee / Sarah Tieck.
     p. cm. -- (Big buddy biographies)
  ISBN 978-1-61714-706-7
  1. Michele, Lea--Juvenile literature. 2. Actors Juvenile literature.--United States--Biography 3. Singers Juvenile
literature.--United States--Biography I. Title.
  PN2287.M6322T54 2010
  792.0'28092--dc22
  [B]
                              2010033803

Contents

Rising Star

Lea Michele is a talented actress and singer. She has appeared in several popular Broadway **musicals**. Lea is best known for starring in the television show *Glee*.

Lea plays Rachel Berry in *Glee*.

5

Lea's parents sometimes attend events with her.

Family Ties

Lea Michele Sarfati was born in New York City, New York, on August 29, 1986. Her parents are Edith and Marc Sarfati. Lea doesn't have any brothers or sisters.

7

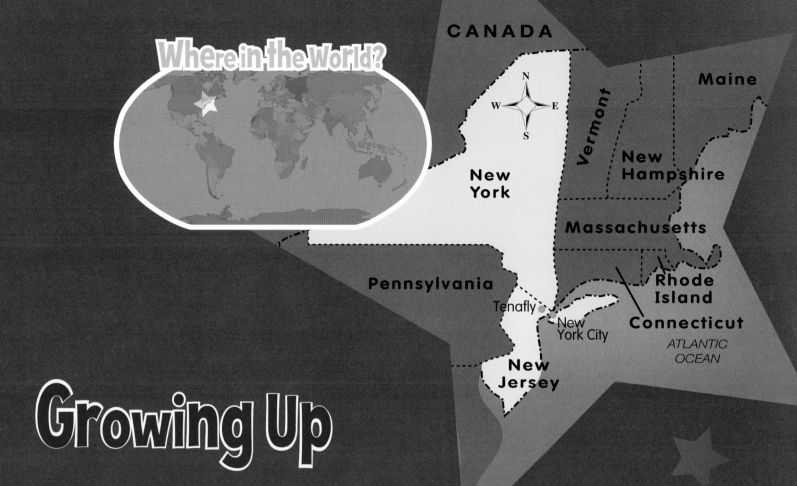

CANADA

Maine

Vermont

New Hampshire

New York

Massachusetts

Pennsylvania

Rhode Island

Tenafly

New York City

Connecticut

ATLANTIC OCEAN

New Jersey

Growing Up

Lea has a large family. In New York, she lived near her grandparents, cousins, aunts, and uncles.

Lea's parents wanted to raise their daughter outside of the city. So, they moved to nearby Tenafly, New Jersey.

Lea was born in an area of New York City called the Bronx.

9

The popular musical *The Phantom of the Opera* is by Andrew Lloyd Webber. He based it on a book by French author Gaston Leroux.

Did you know...

Broadway shows take place in certain theaters in New York City. These shows are considered to be some of the best in the country.

Young Lea went back to New York City to attend Broadway shows. She often went with her friends and their families.

At first, Lea wasn't that interested in the shows. But around age eight, she found she loved the **musical** *The Phantom of the Opera*.

Starting Out

Shortly after, Lea's friend wanted to try out for a **professional** acting part on Broadway. Lea decided she wanted to try out, too.

At the **audition**, Lea sang a song from *The Phantom of the Opera*. She did so well that she got the part of Young Cosette in *Les Misérables*. Her parents were surprised!

Les Misérables is a famous musical. It is based on a book by Victor Hugo.

A Working Actress

Lea was excited to work on Broadway. She began acting in *Les Misérables* in 1995. Lea's family rented an apartment in New York City. But, Lea still lived in Tenafly and went to school there when she could.

People noticed Lea's acting and singing talent. This helped her get more Broadway parts. Soon after her first **role**, Lea acted in the **musical** *Ragtime*. Then in 2001, she got a role in a new musical called *Spring Awakening*.

Lea attended a *Ragtime* show when it returned to Broadway in 2009.

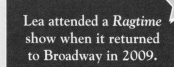

In 2004, Lea began appearing in the musical *Fiddler on the Roof*. Her Broadway costars helped her learn more about performing onstage.

In *Spring Awakening*, Lea starred as a young woman named Wendla.

As a **musical** actor, Lea was very busy. She had to spend time studying her lines. To sing and dance, she had to stay strong and healthy.

During high school, Lea took some time off from acting on Broadway. She was still practicing to star in *Spring Awakening*. But, she had time to attend school. Lea **graduated** in 2004.

Big Break

Spring Awakening opened on Broadway in 2006. It became well known. It even won Tony Awards in 2007! Lea was excited to be part of the show's success.

While starring in Spring Awakening, Lea met television **producer** Ryan Murphy. He was creating a new television show called Glee. He asked Lea to travel to California and try out for the show.

Lea (*right, in the white dress*) was part of a large cast in *Spring Awakening*. In 2007, they performed at the Tony Awards show.

A New Direction

Lea went to her *Glee* **audition** and did her best. Her hard work paid off. Lea got a lead **role**! This was Lea's first lead role on a television show. She found that it was challenging work.

Many people work together to make a television show. To create Lea's look on *Glee*, some workers choose her clothes and makeup.

21

Glee

Glee started **airing** on television in 2009. It became popular very quickly. It is a **musical** television show about a high school singing group, or glee club. The show can be both funny and serious.

Lea plays Rachel Berry. Rachel is a member of the school glee club, New Directions. She and her friends work to prove they are the best singers.

The cast of *Glee* sometimes sings for live audiences.

Lea works with famous actress Jane Lynch (*left*) on *Glee*. Jane plays the cheerleading coach, Sue Sylvester. On the show, Sue and Rachel are enemies!

An Actress's Life

When *Glee* is filming, Lea lives in Los Angeles, California. She works on the television **set** for several hours each day.

When Lea is not working on the show, she attends events and meets fans. Her fans are very excited to meet her!

The cast of *Glee* has won awards for their work. In 2010, the show won a Teen Choice Award.

Off the Screen

In her free time, Lea visits New York City. There, she enjoys hanging out with her family. One of her favorite things to do is eat dinner with them on Sundays. She also works with community groups to help others.

In California, Lea's roommate is her *Glee* costar Dianna Agron. Sometimes they attend events together.

In 2010, Lea was named as a possible winner of an Emmy Award. Even though she didn't win, it was a big honor to be nominated.

Buzz

Lea's fame continues to grow. In 2010, she worked on filming *Glee*'s second season. Fans are excited to see what's next for Lea Michele. Many believe she has a bright **future**!

Snapshot

★**Name**: Lea Michele Sarfati

★**Birthday**: August 29, 1986

★**Birthplace**: New York City, New York

★**Appearances**: *Les Misérables, Ragtime, Fiddler on the Roof, Spring Awakening, Glee*

Important Words

air to show on television or play on the radio.

audition (aw-DIH-shuhn) a trial performance showcasing personal talent as a musician, a singer, a dancer, or an actor.

future (FYOO-chuhr) a time that has not yet occurred.

graduate (GRA-juh-wayt) to complete a level of schooling.

musical a story told with music.

producer a person who oversees the making of a movie, a play, an album, or a radio or television show.

professional (pruh-FEHSH-nuhl) working for money rather than for pleasure.

role a part an actor plays.

set the place where a movie or a television show is recorded.

Web Sites

To learn more about Lea Michele, visit ABDO Publishing Company online. Web sites about Lea Michele are featured on our Book Links page. These links are routinely monitored and updated to provide the most current information available.

www.abdopublishing.com

Index